This Book Belongs To:

Inspired by the real Isabelle and Isaiah
and their imagination.

For information, e-mail mce18@outlook.com.

ISBN:978-1-0692231-1-1

Introduction

In a cozy little town lived two adventurous siblings named Isabelle and Isaiah. Their bright eyes full of wonder and hearts that beat for exploration. One day, as they listened to their grandmother's tales of faraway places, they learned that their family had roots in three special countries: Chile, Eritrea, and Barbados.

Excited by the stories of colorful markets, beautiful landscapes, and warm beaches, Isabelle and Isaiah decided they wanted to visit these magical places for themselves! Their hearts became filled with even more curiosity and they dreamed of exploring Italy's pizzerias, France's charming cafes filled with macaroons, and Japan's fresh sushi.

With their bags packed and maps spread out before them, they set off on a grand adventure ready to try delicious foods and explore incredible sights. Little did they know, each journey would teach them not just about the world but about the unbreakable bond they shared as siblings. And so began their globe trotting adventure!

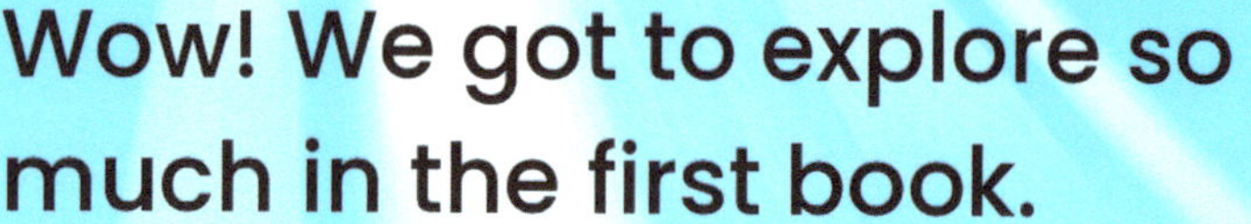

Wow! We got to explore so much in the first book.

Let's explore where our favourite foods come from.

What are your favourite foods?

Are you ready to explore with us?

World map

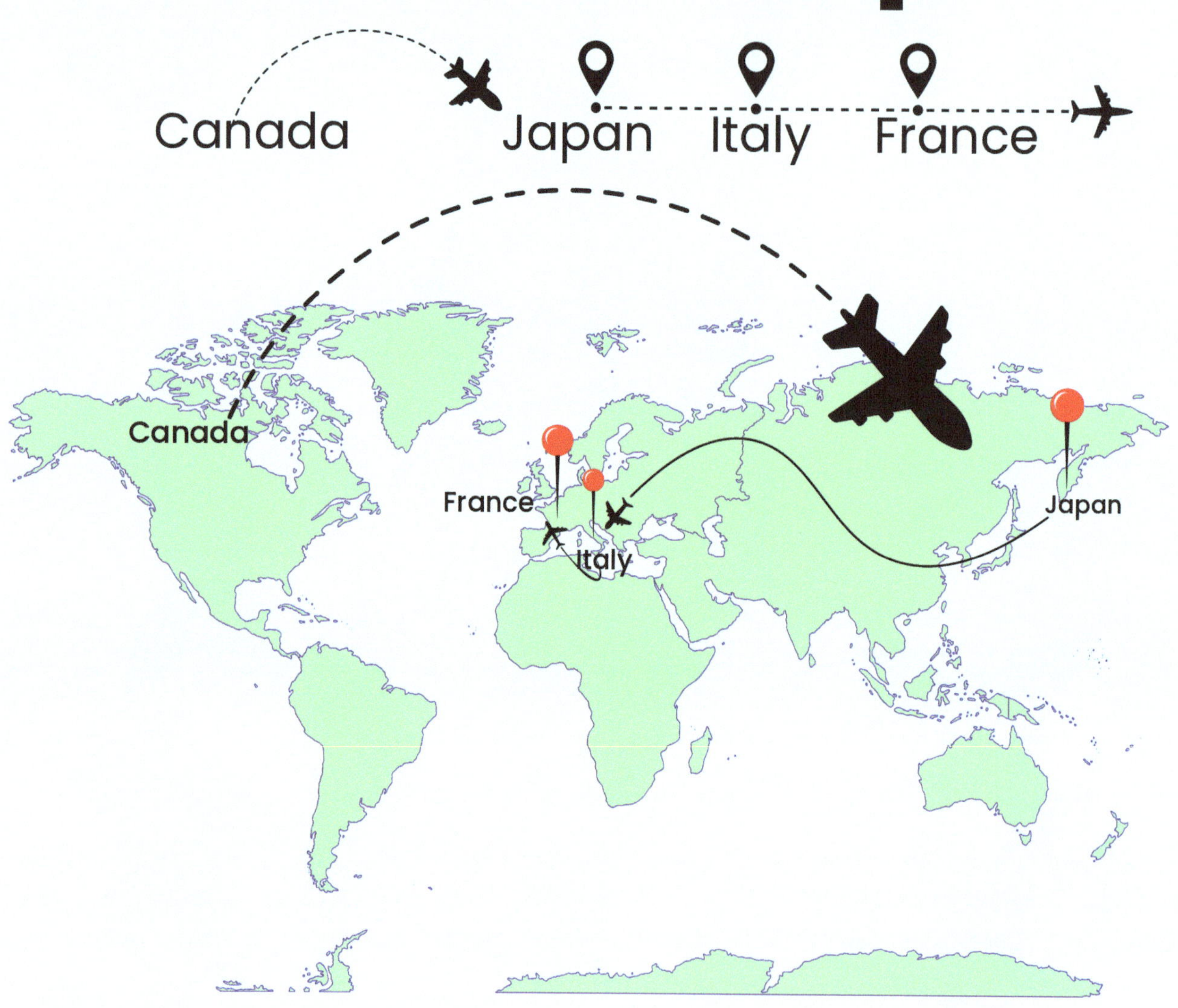

Trace your with your finger!

Isabelle loves sushi and she would love to know where it originates from.

Isaiah shouts out JAPAN!

Let's GO!

JAPAN
Fun fact,
Japan is made up of
many chain islands.

KON'NICHIWA

Japan is located in East Asia, on the Pacific Ocean.

In a peaceful tea house, soft voices are used and women wear plain kimonos while men wear hakamas. Konacha tea is one choice that can be served with a meal called kaiseki. This dish includes sushi, soup, and rice.

Hmm... I could go
for some pizza.
Hey! Where's
pizza from?
ITALY!!!!
Let's explore!!!

Next up, Italy!

ITALY
Fun fact,
Eyeglasses were first invented
in Italy !
ITALIA
ITALIA

Italy is located in Southern Europe and is known for art, fashion, and incredible pastas and pizzas. Also, many tourists come every year to view the ancient ruins in Rome.

We both agree that macaroons are our favourite sweets. Both France and Italy have their own recipes.

I have an idea! Let's go to France!

Did you know,
It took 2 years to build the Eiffel Tower, from 1887-1889.
The Eiffel Tower is 1,083 feet tall!

Bonjour

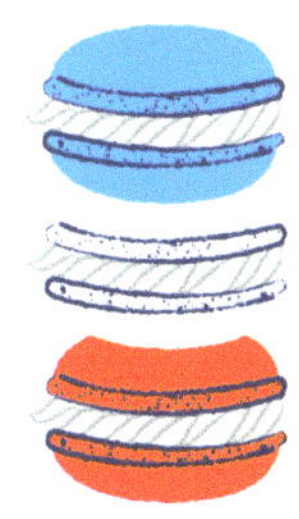

France is located in Western Europe and is famous for their art festivals called “Festival d'Automne à Paris”.

Macaroons are sweet desserts made up of two meringue cookies filled with fruit jams or flavoured buttercream in the middle.

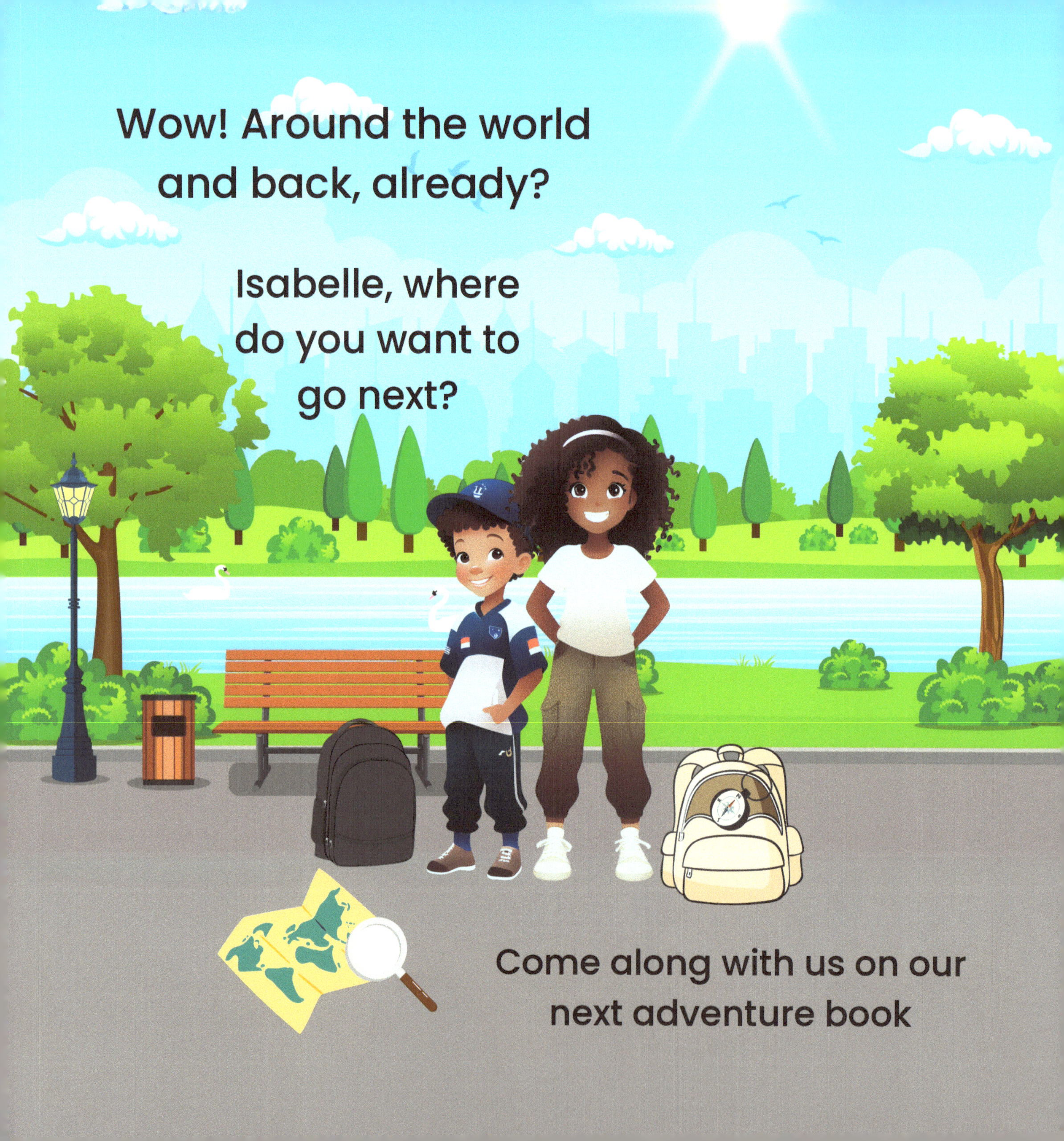

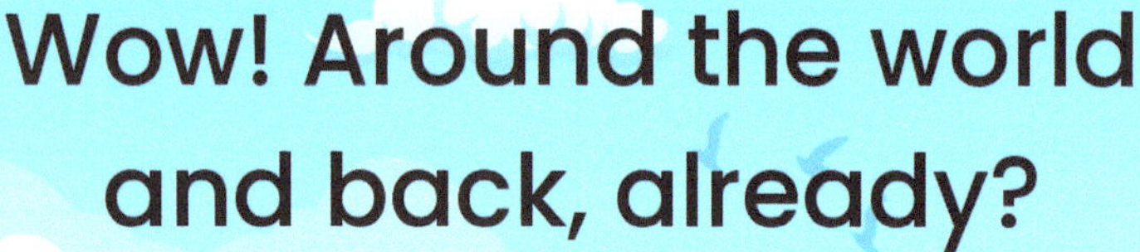

Wow! Around the world and back, already?

Isabelle, where do you want to go next?

Come along with us on our next adventure book

These series of Isabelle and Isaiah's picture books are inspired by and written for children of all ages. These books fulfill children's needs for imagination and curiosity while simultaneously providing a learning experience through adventure. Come travel with us on our next book. Will we be backpacking through the jungle? Or underwater diving in the sea? Maybe on a spaceship to the moon?
You never know! Let's go!

Let's explore in book 3

NEVER
Stop
Exploring

Japan

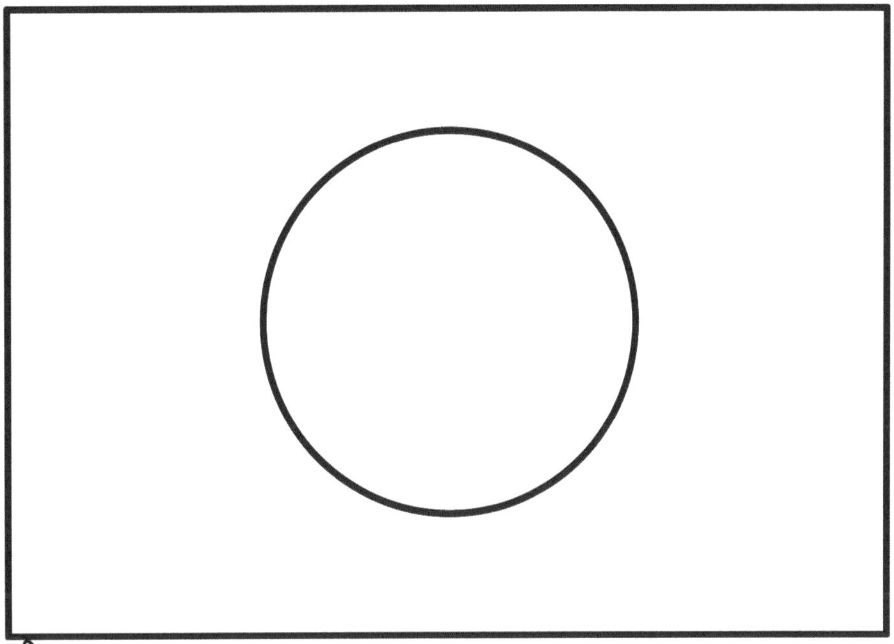

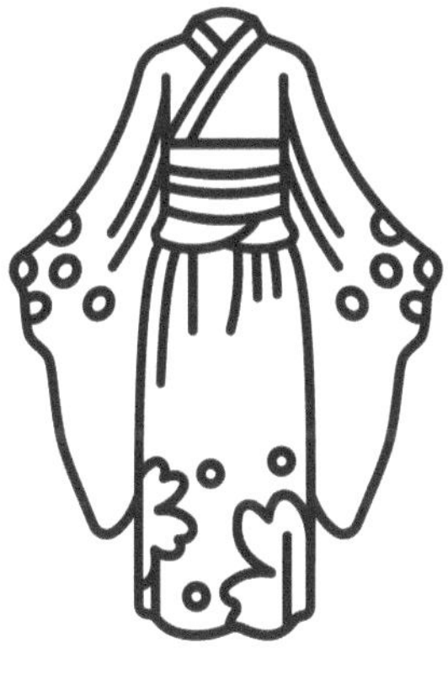

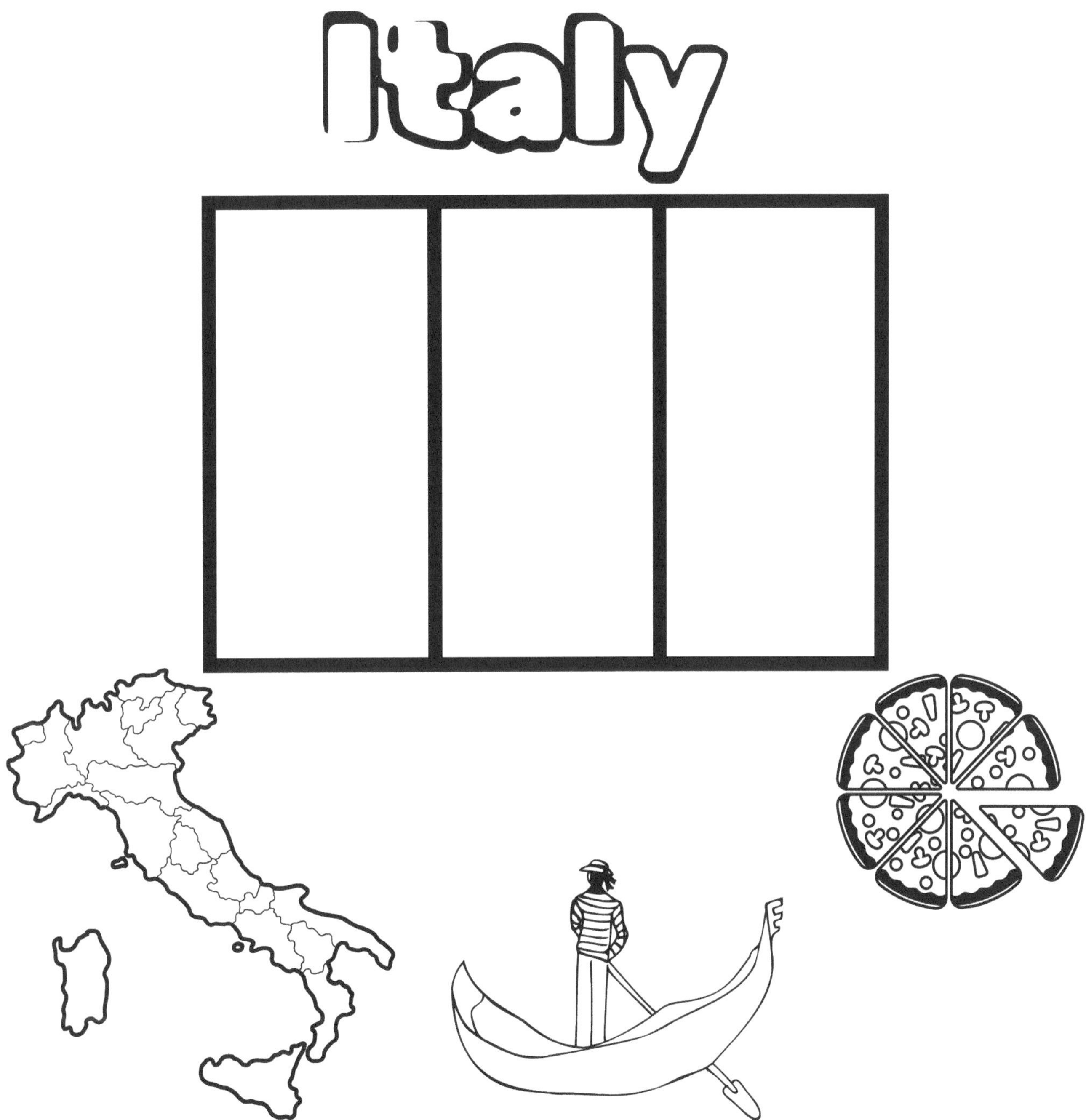
Italy

France
France

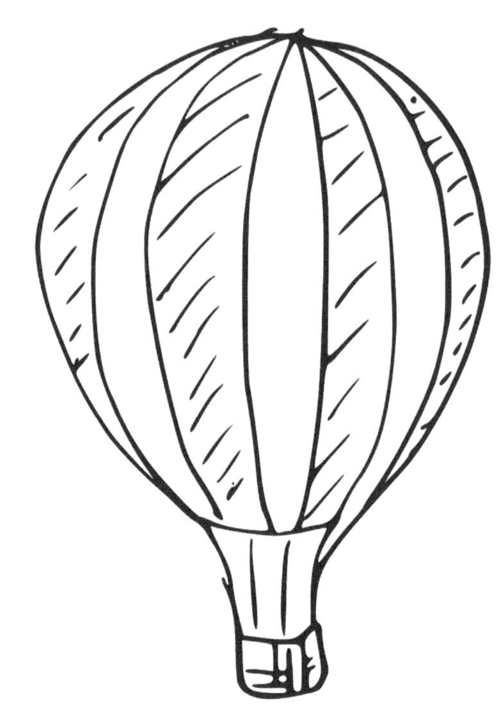

www.ingramcontent.com/pod-product-compliance
Ingram Content Group UK Ltd.
Pitfield, Milton Keynes, MK11 3LW, UK
UKHW060115300726
14090UKWH00002B/199

* 9 7 8 1 0 6 9 2 2 3 1 1 1 *